FALLING UPWARD

A COMPANION JOURNAL

Other Books by Richard Rohr

Falling Upward: A Spirituality for the Two Halves of Life

Immortal Diamond: The Search for Our True Self

FALLING UPWARD

A Spirituality for the Two Halves of Life

A COMPANION JOURNAL

Richard Rohr

JOSSEY-BASS
A Wiley Imprint
www.josseybass.com

Cover design:Rule 29 | rule29.com

Published by Jossey-Bass
A Wiley Imprint
One Montgomery Street, Suite 1200, San Francisco, CA 94104-4594—www.josseybass.com

Jossey-Bass books and products are available through most bookstores. To contact Jossey-Bass directly call our Customer Care Department within the U.S. at 800-956-7739, outside the U.S. at 317-572-3986, or fax 317-572-4002.

Wiley also publishes its books in a variety of electronic formats and by print-on-demand. Not all content that is available in standard print versions of this book may appear or be packaged in all book formats. If you have purchased a version of this book that did not include media that is referenced by or accompanies a standard print version, you may request this media by visiting http://booksupport.wiley.com. For more information about Wiley products, visit us www.wiley.com.

Falling Upward: A Spirituality for the Two Halves of Life: A Companion Journal. ISBN: 978-1-118-42856-6; 978-1-118-42803-0 (ebk); 978-1-118-42853-5 (ebk); 978-1-118-42854-2 (ebk)

Library of Congress Cataloging-in-Publication Data

Rohr, Richard.
  Falling upward : a spirituality for the two halves of life / Richard Rohr.
    p. cm.
    Includes bibliographical references and index.
  ISBN 978-0-470-90775-7 (hardback); 978-1-118-02368-6 (ebk); 978-1-118-02369-3 (ebk); 978-1-118-02370-9 (ebk)
  1. Spiritual formation. 2. Spirituality. I. Title.
  BV4511.R64 2011
  248.4—dc22

2010049429

Printed in the United States of America
FIRST EDITION
PB Printing F10005110_101718

CONTENTS

I can only assume that the continued and engaged response to *Falling Upward*, a book about the spirituality of the two halves of life, reveals that it has named something real. I now meet people who tell me they have read it three times and keep marking it up in new places. But why?

It is surely not a credit to my writing style or my wonderful opinion. Rather, I think the book reveals something with huge pastoral, practical, and therapeutic implications — for individuals, for education, for spiritual growth, and for understanding the development of groups and institutions through two distinct stages: *building our container and finding its contents.* Knowing the difference keeps us from beating our head against the wall and forever asking, "Why is my life not working?" It keeps us from trying to pound round pegs in square holes — or calling other people's pegs wrong.

Others much wiser and broader than I will take this material to other levels of spirituality and psychology, but I think the foundational insight of two major tasks to life and growth — and a necessary crossover point — will hold. That insight is strongly validated by Scripture (law versus Spirit), cultural traditions (education and initiation theories), and now validated by our newly found courage to trust our own experience, even though we might still be afraid to do so. We needed to say it forthrightly, to name what we now realize is obvious. We must start by building our life container, *but it must and will fall apart* (and that is good but also the rub!), and only then do we find the real contents and depths of our own lives.

Knowing about this dynamic also helps us to partly understand the endless conservative-liberal divide in most groups and how both are preserving essential values — though sometimes in the wrong sequence and for too long. You can be a very healthy conservative and also a very unhealthy one, or a very healthy liberal and a very unhealthy one. Both sides need critique and both sides need validation — and at the right time. *Seeming "liberalism" in the young and immature is usually an ego and spiritual disaster; seeming "conservatism" in old folks is often nothing but cognitive rigidity and love of their own status quo and privilege.*

Just as the great spiritual teachers have consistently taught, things are usually not what they seem; and what looks like one thing is often something else entirely. Wisdom lies in knowing the difference, and wisdom is often revealed only in time (Matthew 11:19), as Jesus says.

So more than anything else, I hope the original book, *Falling Upward*, and now its journal can be an exercise in spiritual discernment. This is one of the gifts of the Holy Spirit that Paul briefly lists in 1 Corinthians 12:10 and is similar to the winnowing fork that is central to Odysseus's transformation, and that John the Baptist symbolically puts in the hands of Jesus (Matthew 3:12).

Much of religion has remained stuck and immature because it has not developed this gift of *winnowing* reality, which is what we mean by wisdom: separating essentials from nonessentials, and discerning with subtlety instead of just imposing one-size-fits-all laws. Religion, I am afraid, is notorious for this. Discernment (or *awakening*, as some might call it) is part of what Buddhism focuses on in its own Eight-Fold Path of *wisdom*: right view, right intention, right speech, right action, right livelihood, right effort, right mindfulness, and right concentration. True "rightness" demands a lot more than just obeying laws and following local, recent customs, which tend to pad and affirm the mere ego self.

Paul was trying to get to the same truth when he dedicated two entire letters, Romans and Galatians, to illustrate the clear difference and necessary tension between law and grace, or tradition and Spirit.

One might say that these were Paul's *two most unfortunately unsuccessful letters* in terms of their impact in history. They could have defined Christianity in a truly revolutionary way, but they did not have that effect. Why? Because most Christians were never allowed to know or even were told about the second half of their own lives. They read Paul's letters from a first-half-of-life perspective, with its preoccupation with the concerns of the ego, or from an institutional, clerical perspective, which is finally a waste of time on the full journey.

The same was true for the response to Jesus' sixfold successive listing of, "*It was said . . . and now I say!*" (Matthew 5:21–43). Jesus was pointing to second-half-of-life truths in his Sermon on the Mount, but also summed up the necessary tension at the very beginning: "I have come not to abolish the Law and the Prophets, but to complete them" (5:17), and in the next verse, "The law must not disappear until its very purpose is achieved" (5:18). But once its purpose is achieved and the spiritual values are internalized, law has served its function. You know the rules well enough to know how to break them properly, as the Dalai Lama succinctly puts it. Once the values are built in place, you can let go of the scaffolding.

We now know from schematas like Spiral Dynamics and Integral Theory that it is next to impossible for institutions *as institutions* to operate in a second-half-of-life mode. The best they can do is to protect individuals who are maturing inside of them, which should ideally be the role of wise church leadership: to protect and foster growth toward God even if it means that individuals move beyond or outside their own group. A rare phenomenon, it seems to me, but have you ever noticed how often Jesus tells people to "*Stand up, and go on your way*" (Luke 17:19)? He is into discipleship much more than group belonging. He is into journey more than mere stability. Few have had that kind of maturity or authority, because most of history up to now has been at the tribal and group level of consciousness.

The movement outward as part of maturity is no new pattern. It started with Jesus himself moving to the edge of Judaism; Paul moving to the edge of the new apostolic establishment in Jerusalem; the desert fathers and mothers in the fourth century moving to Egypt, Syria, and Palestine away from the Roman Empire; the nonstop recurrence of religious orders, hermits, anchorites, mystics, reform movements, Protestantism itself, service groups, charismatic movements, and in our time what some call the parachurch phenomenon of "emerging Christianity."

Eventually, like all healthy children, you do have to leave home.

So I welcome you to your own little building project, your own parachurch experiment — not in opposition to anything, or against any idea, or anybody else, but just *doing what you have to do to keep "growing in wisdom, age, and grace"* (Luke 2:40), as Jesus did.

For some sad reason, to keep growing is a threat to an awful lot of people, as the people of Al-Anon have sadly discovered in families suffering from addiction; so we will try to make *growth and journey* a free invitation here, and I hope you can do the same to your friends — not by preaching, but by going the distance yourself — and paying the price yourself!

About the Companion Journal

This Companion Journal grew out of the remarkable interest and enthusiasm for the message of *Falling Upward*, and our desire at the Center for Action and Contemplation to respond to requests from many readers for a resource to help them deepen their experience of the book. A group of over one hundred people in southwest Florida stepped forward to help us create this resource. Two kind members of the facilitation team, Pat Kaufman and Jean Esposito, were instrumental in providing questions, scouting the text for quotations, and creating much of what is in this book. Phil Robers, a leader of the group, and dear friends of the Center for Action and Contemplation also contributed in creating responses to the rich content of *Falling Upward*.

How to Use This Book

This Companion Journal is meant to be used either individually or in groups. We envision that readers will use the quotes, journaling questions, and experiential exercises for reflection, discussion, and journaling.

Although you may certainly dip in and out of chapters or work chronologically through the whole Companion Journal, here are some suggestions for using its elements:

- *Journaling questions*: Writing in response to these questions in each chapter is meant to help you dig deeper into the concepts in the book. We suggest you write the full two pages given for each question in your response so that you explore them fully. (If you want to write more or if there isn't sufficient space in the Companion Journal for your responses, feel free to write in another journal.) You can also use the questions to open discussion in groups.

- *Experiential exercises*: Since spiritual practice is an important part of growth and insight, the experiential exercises at the end of each chapter are designed to help you take your writing and discussions further and integrate them into your life. If you are studying in a group, you can bring stories of your experiences back to the group for discussion and learning together.

- *Quotations for reflection*: Read the quotations scattered throughout each chapter and sit with them. Let their meaning spur thoughts about your experiences or feelings. You can argue with them, question them, and see how they are true for you. In groups, they (and your reflections about them) are great conversation starters.

RICHARD ROHR, OFM
NOVEMBER 2012

FALLING UPWARD

CHAPTER 1

The Two Halves of Life

The task of the first half of life is to create a proper container *for one's life and answer the first essential questions: "What makes me significant?" "How can I support myself?" and "Who will go with me? " (p. 1)*

Think about your childhood faith. What do you remember believing? What was important to you? How has your childhood faith changed? How do you respond to Fr. Richard's call to make your own "discoveries of Spirit"?

_____

_____

_____

_____

_____

_____

_____

_____

_____

_____

_____

_____

_____

_____

_____

_____

_____
_____
_____
_____
_____
_____

"The task of the first half of life is to create a proper container for one's life and answer the first essential questions: 'What makes me significant?' 'How can I support myself?' and 'Who will go with me?'" (p. 1)

_____
_____
_____
_____
_____
_____
_____
_____
_____
_____
_____

In the context of the security structures created to define tribes, loyalty, and identity, does the question, "Is that all there is?" resonate with your experience? If so, how?

_____

_____

_____

_____

_____

_____

_____

_____

_____

_____

_____

_____

_____

_____

_____

_____

As you reflect on your life, do you see deeper meaning in your youthful life experiences than you did when they were happening? What changes do you feel called to make now that will free you up to living a larger life on behalf of the world?

"*If change and growth are not programmed into your spirituality, if there are not serious warnings about the blinding nature of fear and fanaticism, your religion will* always *end up worshiping the status quo and protecting your present ego position and personal advantage — as if it were God!*" (p. 11)

How would you define "both-and" thinking? Using Gandhi, Anne Frank, Martin Luther King Jr., Mother Teresa, and Nelson Mandela as examples, what do you think you might have to give up to be a truly both-and thinker?

_____

_____

_____

_____

_____

_____

_____

_____

_____

_____

_____

_____

_____

_____

_____

_____

_____

_____

_____

_____

_____

_____

"You can only see and understand the earlier stages from the wider perspective of the later stages... If you have, in fact, deepened and grown 'in wisdom, age, and grace' (Luke 2:52), you are able to be patient, inclusive, and understanding of all the previous stages." (p. 9)

_____

_____

_____

_____

_____

_____

_____

_____

_____

In what ways could Jesus' command to "change your mind" (Mark 1:15) affect your personal journey? Spend time thinking about the difficult situations and relationships in your life that are difficult now. How might they be challenging and inviting you to change your mind?

Experiential Exercises

• Treat yourself to a slow walk through your neighborhood. Recognize the gift of life that your breath is, and take time to think about your breathing as you walk. Notice things of beauty that might never have appeared beautiful to you in the past. Notice things that you would not usually think of as special. How are you seeing them differently? Pick up a stone or a stick, and let it leave its imprint on your mind and heart. Think about where this object has been through time and history. When you return home, write about your experience, and call a friend to share what you have just experienced.

"We all want and need various certitudes, constants, and insurance policies at every stage of life. But we have to be careful, or they totally take over and become all-controlling needs, keeping us from further growth . . . *The most common one liner in the Bible is 'Do not be afraid.'"* (p. 6)

• Move through the next week paying great attention to the world around you. At work, notice how inclusively people treat each other, and look for psychologically and spiritually mature behaviors. When you are waiting in a line, watch for the presence or

"The task of the second half of life is, quite simply, to find the actual contents that this container was meant to hold and deliver . . . The second half of life can hold some new wine because by then there should be some new wineskins, some tested ways of holding our lives together." (pp. 1–2)

absence of patience or understanding around you. Observe families, and see if the adults show signs of compassion and empathy to the children. In your exposure to the media, watch for signs of either-or or both-and thinking. In the context of your spiritual life, listen and watch for ways that you might grow in wisdom, age, and grace. At the end of the week, make a list of your observations. What have the moments of compassion and maturity called forth from you? What about the moments that don't offer these qualities? Spend time thinking about how you could use these observations to improve the quality of your relationships and interactions.

CHAPTER 2

The Hero and the Heroine's Journey

A "hero" now is largely about being bold, muscular, rich, famous, talented, or "fantastic" by himself, and often for himself, whereas the classic hero is one who "goes the distance," whatever that takes, and then has plenty left over for others. True heroism serves the common good, or it is not really heroism at all. (p. 20)

What does "Divine DNA" (p. 18) mean to you? Are you in touch with your Divine DNA? If so, how did you become aware of it? How does it affect you or motivate you to act? If you are not in touch, what can you do to make a connection? Who or what might be able to help?

Over your life journey, when have you been called to go beyond your comfort zone, how have these challenges affected your spiritual growth? What experiences or resources do people need to make a leap of faith more conceivable for them?

~ "The very first sign of the potential hero's journey is that he or she must leave home, the familiar. If you have spent many years building your particular tower of success and self-importance — your personal 'salvation project,' as Thomas Merton called it — or have successfully constructed your own superior ethnic group, religion, or 'house,' you won't want to leave it." Can you identify a wound in your life that has opened you to a whole new understanding? How has it shaped the person you have become? Can you identify a major dilemma or life experience that is still trying to change you? How might you invite it to do so intentionally?

_____

_____

_____

_____

_____

_____

_____

_____

"I wonder if we have that real . . . sense of destiny, call, and fate that led Odysseus to leave father, wife, and son for a second journey. That is the very same obedience . . . that Jesus scandalously talks about in several places." (p. 22)

How would describe the difference between your current life situation and what Fr. Richard calls your "actual life"? Do you have a sense that there is a deeper movement beneath the surface of your everyday tasks? Can you describe what Fr. Richard calls "what you are doing while you are doing what you're doing"?

_____

_____

_____

_____

_____

_____

_____

_____

_____

_____

_____

_____

_____

"Jesus was not a nuclear family man at all, by any common definition! What led so many saints to seek the "will of God" first and above their own? What has led so many Peace Corps workers, missionaries, and skilled people to leave their countries for difficult lands and challenges?" Make a list of those in your life who have shared with you the wisdom they have gained from their life lessons. How has their wisdom affected you? When you are given the opportunity to pass life lessons on to others, what questions would you ask of the person to help you to know what he or she needs?

_____

_____

_____

_____

_____

_____

_____

_____

_____

_____

"Unless you build your first house well, you will never leave it. To build your house well is, ironically, to be nudged beyond its doors." (p. 23)

Experiential Exercises

• Get a long piece of paper and crayons or colored pencils. Spend time reflecting on your hero's journey thus far. Picture your life as a river and yourself as a leaf floating on that river. Begin at the far left of your paper, and draw the river of your life with your leaf following its path. As you visualize times in your life, use the drawing to illustrate changes you have experienced. Are there times when your life river becomes very shallow? Or when it is wide and deep? Are there times when your river is roiled and muddy? Or crystal clear? Does the river become very narrow, or do you approach rapids or steep waterfalls that your leaf must master? Are there times when the river's flow is calm and peaceful? Does your river sometimes twist and bend sharply? Is it straight and strong at times? Draw all those changes in the river to indicate the differences in its flow.

• Note the times when you were called on to leave home, where you were led, how it felt. Note times when you were able to sense God's presence and those when you had more difficulty doing so. As you sit with your drawing, think about where you are now on your hero's journey. Write a prayer for continued guidance and the willingness to leave home again.

"We cannot rush the process; we can only carry out each stage of our lives to the best of our ability—and then we no longer need to do it anymore!" (p. 24)

• Play some music that inspires you to move. Dance if you are inclined, but even the most subtle of movements will do. Experience the places in your body where you are holding on to things that keep you from embracing a thriving existence. Breathe into those places. Invite them to your awareness. Name them here, along with the feelings they evoke, and commit to holding it in awareness.

CHAPTER 3

The First Half
of Life

 *You need a very strong
container to hold the contents
and contradictions that arrive
later in life. You ironically need
a very strong ego structure to let
go of your ego.* (p. 26)

Write about a necessary fall that you've experienced—for example, a loss of job, reputation, self-image, a relationship, or a moral failure that you had to own up to. Did that experience teach you more about balance? About yourself? About God? What did you learn, and what more do you think you have yet learn? If you have never let yourself fall or perceived you were never allowed to fall, what impact do you think that is having on your life?

"We are parts of social and family ecosystems that are rightly structured to keep us from falling but also, more important, to show us how to fall and also how to learn from that very falling . . . You learn how to recover from falling by falling!" (p. 28)

How would you define unconditional love? Name someone who loved you that way, and describe how you felt. Now name someone who offered conditional or demanding love, and describe that experience. Contrast the two and how they affected you. Do you see value for yourself in having been loved in these different ways?

Name the loyal soldier in you. What is he or she trying to protect or obtain? Spend some time thinking about the parallel between your loyal soldier and the elder son in Jesus' parable of the Prodigal Son. What might your loyal soldier keep you from knowing or experiencing? What kind of ritual might you devise to discharge your loyal soldier (your career accomplishments after retirement, your military experiences after war, your full-time parental devotion after the empty nest)? How might others play a role in that ritual? Make a journal entry after you have performed it to describe how it felt. How will you celebrate the "death of the false self and the . . . birth of the soul"?

"The voice of our loyal soldier gets us through the first half of life safely, ... to learn the sacred 'no' to ourselves that gives us dignity, identity, direction, significance, and boundaries. We *must* learn these lessons to get off to a good start! ... Paradoxically, your loyal soldier gives you so much security and validation that you may confuse his voice with the very voice of God." As you reflect on your life, can you identify some of the illusions that God has undone for you? Were you aware of what was happening at the time? How has your life changed as a result? Do these experiences illustrate for you the idea that "the best word for God is actually *Mystery*"?

_____

_____

_____

_____

_____

_____

_____

_____

"St. John of the Cross taught that God has to work in the soul in secret and in darkness, because if we fully knew what was happening, and what Mystery/transformation/God/grace will eventually ask of us, we would either try to take charge or stop the whole process." (Gerald May, The Dark Night of the Soul. quoted on pp. 50–51)

Experiential Exercises

• Because the contemplative mind can accept Mystery, it can receive things just as they are and let them teach us. This week, seek out a quiet, sacred place at home or outside where you are able to sit undisturbed for a period of time. Be fully present in this sacred space for a set period of time each day. Repeat a word or phrase that holds meaning for you

"Without that necessary separation, order itself... will often feel like a kind of 'salvation.' It has been the most common and bogus substitute for the real liberation offered by mature religion... But I am not here to say either-or. I am here to say both-and." (pp. 38–39)

to settle your mind into the presence of God. If thoughts intrude, use your word or phrase to bring you back to quiet. Once this practice is part of your schedule, observe how your ability to "hold creative tensions" deepens. As you reflect on your key life experiences, ask yourself these questions that Fr. Richard poses in "Everything Belongs."

- *"What is the message in this for me?*
- *What's the gift in this for me?*
- *How is God in this event?*
- *Where is God in this suffering?"*

"There is a deeper voice of God, which you must learn to hear and obey *in the second half of life. It will sound an awful lot like the voices of risk, of trust, of surrender, of soul, of 'common sense,' of destiny, of love, of an intimate stranger, of your deepest self."* (p. 48)

• Reflect on your capacity for giving and receiving love. Consider a relationship where it is difficult to give love and one where it is difficult to receive love. In the relationship where offering love is challenging, consider the story you carry that makes it difficult to love. Invite yourself to question that story. In the relationship where receiving love is challenging, consider the story that diminishes your openness, and invite yourself to question it. Hold these people in your heart during your prayer time. See them surrounded by love and you surrounded by love. Repeat this practice, and notice any urging you feel toward greater openness.

CHAPTER 4

The Tragic Sense of Life

Life is not, nor ever has been, a straight line forward ... Life is characterized much more by exception and disorder than by total or perfect order. Life, as the biblical tradition makes clear, is both loss and renewal, death and resurrection, chaos and healing at the same time; life seems to be a collision of opposites. (p. 54)

~ Journal about your reaction to the statement that "life is inherently tragic." What does that mean to you? How does faith help (or not help) you deal with the contradictions of life?

_____

_____

_____

_____

_____

_____

_____

_____

_____

_____

_____

_____

"The Gospel is able to accept that life is tragic, but then graciously added that we can survive and will even grow from this tragedy. This is the great turnaround! It all depends on whether we are willing to see down as up." (p. 58)

Have you sought God's compassion and forgiveness for issues in your life? Describe how it feels to embrace that forgiveness. Did the experience of seeking forgiveness move you to "trust and seek and love God" more deeply? If you have not yet allowed yourself to accept God's absolute forgiveness, write a letter to God about the forgiveness you seek and ask God's help in becoming ready to receive it.

_____

_____

_____

_____

_____

_____

_____

_____

_____

_____

_____

_____

_____

"Our mistakes are something to be pitied and healed much more than hated, denied, or perfectly avoided. I do not think you should get rid of your sin until you have learned what it has to teach you." (p. 61)

Do you gravitate toward the "never-broken, always-applicable rules and patterns" of life? Describe how you deal with things that do not fit "the universal mold." By what methods have you been able to free yourself of the need to adhere to specific principles in every situation?

"Organized religion has not
been known for its
inclusiveness or for being
very comfortable with
diversity. Yet pluriformity,
multiplicity, and diversity
is the only world there is! It
is rather amazing that we
can miss, deny, or ignore
what is in plain sight
everywhere." *(p. 60)*

Do you agree that even our sin/error has something to teach us? Could there be such a thing as "necessary transgressions" as we seem to see in the Adam and Eve story? Write about a lesson that you have learned through acknowledgment of a destructive pattern in your life.

_____

_____

_____

_____

_____

_____

_____

_____

_____

_____

_____

_____

What does the term *necessary suffering* mean to you? What is an example of it in your life? Describe a time when the awareness of your connection to the big picture helped you cope with failure and loss. Does the context of your place within the larger whole help you absorb it?

_____

_____

_____

_____

_____

_____

_____

_____

_____

_____

_____

_____

_____

_____

_____

_____

_____

_____

_____

_____

_____

_____

_____

"The tragic sense of life is not unbelief, pessimism, fatalism, or cynicism. It is just ultimate and humiliating realism, *which for some reason demands a lot of forgiveness of almost everything. Faith is simply to trust the real, and to trust that God is found within it—even before we change it." (p. 63)*

Experiential Exercises

- Fr. Richard writes, "Jesus had no trouble with the exceptions, whether they were prostitutes, drunkards, Samaritans, lepers, Gentiles, tax collectors, or wayward sheep." Look for the "exceptions" in your everyday life this week. Watch for your responses to those who fall outside your sense of what is normal or right or good. Invite the Christ mind to clarify your awareness and understanding. Consider how you might reach out to learn more about a person or population you have previously judged as abnormal or separate.

> *"It is those creatures and those humans who are on the edge of what we have defined as normal, proper, or good who often have the most to teach us. They tend to reveal the shadow and mysterious side of things."*
> (p. 55)

- Fold a large sheet of paper in half horizontally. Open it back up, and make two columns, one labeled "bad stuff" and the other "good stuff." Sit and think about your life as a tragedy. Focus on the difficult and painful events: times of loss, hopelessness, crises of faith, and suffering. List these situations in phrase form in the "bad stuff" column. Now take a short walk and invite yourself

"Judeo-Christian salvation history is an integrating, using, and forgiving of this tragic sense of life. *Judeo-Christianity includes the problem inside the solution . . . The genius of the biblical revelation is that it refuses to deny the dark side of things, but forgives failure and integrates falling to achieve its only promised wholeness.*" (p. 59)

into the "Great Turn-around." As you walk, hold these difficulties in your heart. Invite an awareness of how they have served your greater good. Can you find the benevolence of difficulty? Now consider your life's greatest moments. Focus on successes, love, achievements, the times when your life has felt connected, and you were in the flow. Write these in the "good stuff" column. Do you see a correlation between your difficulties and your achievements? Do you see how in some instances, overcoming your difficulties has made the good stuff possible or how what was good at one time had to be surpassed for future good to come? Hold gratitude in your heart for what appears as good and what appears as bad.

CHAPTER 5

Stumbling over the Stumbling Stone

> *You will and you must 'lose' at something. This is the only way that Life-Fate-God-Grace-Mystery can get you to change, let go of your egocentric preoccupations, and go on the further and larger journey.*
>
> *(pp. 65–66)*

~ Fr. Richard writes, "If you are on any classic 'spiritual schedule,' some event, person, death, idea, or relationship will enter your life that you simply cannot deal with, using your present skill set, your acquired knowledge, or your strong willpower." Write about a time when a situation took you beyond your resources to deal with it. Did the experience bring you to a new awareness of your capacity for surrender? Did you feel free when you realized you were not in charge of the falling?

_____

_____

_____

_____

_____

_____

_____

_____

_____

_____

_____

"*There must be, and, if we are honest, there always will be at least one situation in our lives that we cannot fix, control, explain, change, or even understand.*" (p. 68)

Write about a time in your life when failure and humiliation forced you to look for answers where you would not have otherwise. Describe what you discovered.

"If we seek spiritual heroism ourselves, the old ego is just back in control under a new name. There would not really be any change at all, but only disguise. Just bogus 'self-improvement,' on our own terms." (p. 66)

What does being "out of the driver's seat" or "giving up control to the Real Guide" mean to you? Have you had a strong plan in your life that eventually proved to be insufficient? Describe the significantly new self you found in reaching for the "real source, the deep well, . . . the constantly flowing stream."

_____

_____

_____

_____

_____

_____

_____

_____

_____

_____

_____

_____

_____

_____

"We must actually be out of the driver's seat for a while, or we will never learn how to give up control to the Real Guide. It is the necessary pattern. This kind of falling is what I mean by necessary suffering." *(p. 66)*

When has suffering opened new spaces in your life for learning and loving? If you find this concept challenging, write out a memory of suffering, watching for any new insights you receive about these painful experiences. Write them down for future reflection.

"If you do not do the task of the first half of life well, you have almost no ability to rise up from the stumbling stone. You just stay down and defeated, or you waste your time kicking against the goad." *(p. 71)*

The goad that St. Francis learned not to kick against is defined as "the symbol of both the encouragement forward and our needless resistance to it, which only wounds us further." What do you kick against in your life? What might accepting your goad teach you? How might such acceptance help you to grow?

_____

_____

_____

_____

_____

_____

_____

_____

_____

_____

_____

_____

Experiential Exercises

• In the week ahead, pay attention to your life. Use all of your senses as you observe people and events with new eyes. Pay attention to things that you may never have noticed before. Look especially at faces and read what they say. As you touch others, perhaps as you shake hands, truly feel the person's grasp, sensing what these hands may have accomplished. Amid all your experiences, listen closely for the still, small voice of the Spirit within you. Speak more gently and with more humility. Notice any effect your gentleness may have. Write a prayer or a poem that describes what you have learned.

• Think back on your experiences of precious things that you have lost and then found. Recall how you felt when you realized the loss — and when the lost item was found. Remember those inner celebrations you've experienced. Write a "lost and found story" about your life.

"It seems that in the spiritual world, we do not really find something until we first lose it, ignore it, miss it, long for it, choose it, and personally find it again — but now on a new level." (p. 67)

CHAPTER 6

Necessary Suffering

 Carl Jung said that so much unnecessary suffering comes into the world because people will not accept the "legitimate suffering" that comes from being human. (p. 73)

~ Why is it easy and self-aggrandizing to "throw rocks from the outside"? What kinds of experiences—in prayer, community, service, relationships—might foster "unlocking spiritual things from inside?"

_____

_____

_____

_____

_____

_____

_____

_____

_____

_____

_____

_____

_____

Describe what you have observed in nature that you would call necessary suffering. Does seeing necessary suffering as part of the natural order of things have an impact on you as you observe the suffering in your own life?

_____

_____

_____

_____

_____

_____

_____

_____

_____

_____

_____

_____

_____

_____

_____

_____

_____

"Necessary suffering goes on every day, seemingly without question . . . Most of nature seems to totally accept major loss, gross inefficiency, mass extinctions, and short life spans as the price of life at all." (p. 77)

How do you use your freedom to say yes or no to spiritual growth? Are you open to exploring your own dying, stumbling, mistakes, and falling? What prevents your doing this? What difference could the willingness make in your journey?

~~~ Describe your own experience with the "crab bucket syndrome" (when you try to crawl out but others pull you back in) within your family, social network, religious community, or work environment. What affects your ability to move to the second journey? Does the voice of the collective affect your spiritual choices? Name specific situations that you perceived to hinder your forward movement. How can you change those situations?

_____

_____

_____

_____

_____

_____

_____

_____

_____

_____

"As we move into the second half of life, ... we are very often at odds with our natural family and the 'dominant consciousness' of our cultures ... Many people are kept from mature religion because of the pious, immature, or rigid expectations of their first-half-of-life family."
(pp. 82–83)

What does the spiritual greats' motto, "Leave home to find it," mean to you? List your favorite "homes" — your validations, securities, illusions, prejudices, or hurts. Why are they (or were they) so difficult to let go? Is there a "home" you still need to leave? Write a before-and-after scenario for yourself that exemplifies your spiritual growth.

_____

_____

_____

_____

_____

_____

_____

_____

_____

_____

_____

_____

"It takes a huge push, much self-doubt, and some degree of separation for people to find their own soul and their own destiny apart from what Mom and Dad always wanted them to be and do." *(p. 83)*

Try to describe your false self, your roles, titles, personal images. What feelings are evoked when you consider the death of your false self? What is your understanding of "the pearl of great price," and how might you reveal where it is hidden within you already?

_____

_____

_____

_____

_____

_____

_____

_____

_____

_____

_____

_____

_____

_____

Experiential Exercises

• Sit with your Bible or another holy book. Ask the Holy Spirit for eyes to see and ears to hear the Word of God, and open the book randomly and begin to read. As you read, mark passages that speak to you. Use different colored highlighters to indicate how specific verses speak to different areas of your life: your

"Your True Self is who you objectively are from the beginning, in the mind and heart of God, 'the face you had before you were born,' as the Zen masters say. It is your substantial self, your absolute identity, which can be neither gained nor lost." (p. 86)

family and friends, your work, worship, community activities, and so on. Look for patterns in what you mark as you read. When you are finished, review the sets of passages that are highlighted in the same color and think about where they have taken you that is new, good, and much more spacious.

• Call to mind a story or a parable about someone's falling and being redeemed. Choose someone in the story to identify with. Perhaps begin as the hero. Allow yourself to play out the role of the person. Ask whether you would have made the same choices. Feel the creative tension in the story; think about the truth

"The resolution of earthly embodiment and divinization is what I call incarnational mysticism . . . *Only that which is limited and even dies grows in value and appreciation; it is the spiritual version of supply and demand."* (pp. 78–79)

it offers to you. What qualities allowed the person to fall, and what allowed the person to be redeemed? Now choose another character in the story, perhaps the foil. How are these two stories similar or different? Write in your journal about the characteristics of each that you would like to see revealed in you, and characteristics of each you would like to have redeemed in you.

CHAPTER 7

Home and Homesickness

 Life is a luminous pause between two great mysteries, which themselves are one.

(Carl Jung, quoted on p. 88)

⤳ Consider Odysseus's oar that an inland wayfarer saw as a winnowing fan. What things in your life are "chaff" or nonessential? How can you eliminate or minimize them? What things in your life are "wheat"—essentials that give deeper meaning? What can you do to emphasize those things to a greater degree?

_____

_____

_____

_____

_____

_____

_____

_____

_____

_____

_____

_____

_____

_____

_____

_____

_____

_____

"Odysseus's oar 'had become a tool for inner work, a means for knowing the difference between the wheat and chaff, essentials and nonessentials, which is precisely the turn toward discernment and subtlety that we come to in the second half of life.' " (p. 94)

Make a list of times in your life when you experienced an inner restlessness, and use the list to ponder the following questions: What were the circumstances surrounding the times you felt restless? Are there common trends underlying these times? Do these point you toward an *inner drive and necessity* that help to reveal your true self?

"*There is an inherent and desirous dissatisfaction that both sends and draws us forward, and it comes from our original and radical union with God.*" (p. 89)

~ Does thinking of your soul as a homing device or inner compass that guides you toward home make sense to you? Do you think that God would plant a desire in us for what God already wants to give us?

_____

_____

_____

_____

_____

_____

_____

_____

_____

_____

_____

_____

_____

_____

"The self-same moment that we find God in ourselves, we also find ourselves inside God, and this is the full homecoming, according to Teresa of Avila." Do you agree that evil is more about superficiality and blindness than about consciously malicious deeds? How have you seen that in your own life? Or in the life of others?

Have you found that God is in the depths of everything, especially in our failings and failures? If so, can you give an example that would illustrate this idea?

_____

_____

_____

_____

_____

_____

_____

_____

_____

_____

_____

_____

_____

"Heaven/union/love now emerge from within us, much more than from a mere belief system or any belonging system, which largely remains on the outside of the self." What does it mean to say that the Spirit works largely in secret? Do you believe that the Spirit "keeps us connected and safe inside an already existing flow"? Can you think of some examples that would help you to explain that to others?

Experiential Exercises

• Fr. Richard says, "If we go to the depths of anything, we will begin to knock upon something substantial, 'real,' and with a timeless quality to it. We will move . . . to an actual inner *knowing*. This is especially true if we have ever (1) loved deeply, (2) accompanied someone through the mystery of dying, (3) or stood in genuine life-changing *we* before mystery, time, or beauty." Recall a situation when you have experienced life at a very deep level. Close your eyes, and spend several minutes recreating the situation in as much vivid detail as you can. Based on that experience, ask yourself what things in life are certain. List them, and reconsider the list every day over the next week. Record your insights at the end of the week.

> *"The Holy Spirit is that aspect of God that works largely from within and 'secretly,' at 'the deepest level of our desiring.' . . . We never 'create' or earn the Spirit; we discover this inner abiding as we learn to draw upon our deepest inner life." (p. 90)*

• Identify a "wisdom person" or "elder" whom you know who lives life in deeper communion. Conduct an interview with him or her using some questions

"The gift of living in our time . . . is that we are more and more discovering that the sciences, particularly physics, astrophysics, anthropology, and biology, are confirming many of the deep intuitions of religion." (p. 93)

you've written to understand his or her journey and experience. Share some about where you see yourself on your spiritual journey and seek his or her experience and reflections. Take notes on the conversation, and select ideas to integrate into your life.

CHAPTER 8

Amnesia and the Big Picture

 We all seem to suffer from a tragic case of mistaken identity. Life is a matter of becoming fully and consciously who we already are, but it is a self that we largely do not know. (p. 97)

How would you describe your "True Self"? What do you think it takes to discover your True Self? How has your religion served you well as teacher and guide in finding your True Self? How has it not served you well?

_____

_____

_____

_____

_____

_____

_____

_____

_____

_____

_____

_____

If you have ever felt it necessary to perform in a "worthiness contest" (anything where the issue itself is not that important but is merely a staging event for you to prove yourself as good, acceptable, smart, competent, or superior)? What did it feel like? Think about the arbitrary "rules" of the contest and how you had to perform. What did you achieve, and what, if anything, did you have to sacrifice to achieve it?

"We forget or deny things that are just too good to be true. *The ego clearly prefers an economy of merit, where we can divide the world into winners and losers, to any economy of grace, where merit or worthiness loses all meaning.*" (p. 104)

~ What does the "prison-house of the false self" mean for you? What do you need to unlearn from your religious education or upbringing to free yourself from it?

_____

_____

_____

_____

_____

_____

_____

_____

_____

_____

_____

_____

~ What are the "little kingdoms" you have created to replace the union with God where you cannot yet abide? How do they inhibit your experience of union with God now?

_____

_____

_____

_____

_____

_____

_____

_____

_____

_____

_____

_____

_____

"How could anyone enjoy
the 'perfect happiness' of
any heaven if she knew her
loved ones were not there,
or were being tortured for
all eternity?" *(p. 101)*

Fr. Richard writes, "No one is in hell unless that individual himself or herself chooses a final aloneness and separation . . . It is interesting to me that the official church has never declared a single person to be in hell, not even Judas, Hitler, or Stalin." Can you see when you are choosing union, and when you are choosing separation? How might this statement alter your concepts of heaven and hell?

_____

_____

_____

_____

_____

_____

_____

_____

_____

_____

*"Why would Jesus' love be
so unconditional while he
was in the world, and
suddenly become totally
conditional after death?
. . . Belief in heaven and
hell is meant to maintain
freedom on all sides, with
God being the most free of
all, to forgive and include,
to heal and to bless even
God's seeming 'enemies.'"*
(pp. 102–103)

_____

_____

_____

_____

_____

_____

_____

Experiential Exercises

• Consider what you have learned and begun to question as you have read *Falling Upward*. Meditate on your personal definitions of False Self and True Self and your concepts of heaven and hell. Pay special attention this week to how you respond to conversations or behaviors when you are among friends, family, and strangers from the perspective of heaven and hell as being NOW. Walk through your week noticing whether you experience yourself in heaven or in hell moment by moment. Notice how your behaviors in these two places are different and whether others respond to you differently when your experience is one or the other. Record your observations in your journal.

"If you go to heaven alone, wrapped in your private worthiness, it is by definition not heaven. If your notion of heaven is based on exclusion of anybody else, then it is by definition not heaven."
(p. 101)

• Jesus told us to love our enemies. Are you ready for the challenge of following this commandment? Make a list of people you find challenging and those whom you believe find you challenging. During this week, explore what it would take to love these people.

"A person who has found his or her true self has learned how to live in the big picture, as a part of deep time and all of history. This change of frame and venue is called living in 'the kingdom of God' by Jesus."
(p. 101)

Then, if you are willing, concentrate on at least one person from the list. When you encounter this person, be present to him or her as love (not affection or sentiment, but open-heartedness and invitation). How does it change you to open your heart to a person you find challenging? What do you risk by doing this? What do you gain? Then try it with a few others on your list, and write about what you learn from this experience.

CHAPTER 9

A Second Simplicity

 I was always being moved toward greater differentiation and larger viewpoints, and simultaneously toward a greater inclusivity in my ideas, a deeper understanding of people, and a more honest sense of justice. God always became bigger and led me to bigger places. If God could "include" and allow, then why not I?

(p. 107)

Do you see a need for an increase in inclusivity in your church or spiritual home? How about in the rest of your life? How has this changed as your spirituality has matured? Does "otherness" or newness threaten you? Why do you think it does threaten so many people? Do you feel safe with your God? Free? Loved? Trustful? Invited? If not, write about why that might be so, and who God is to you.

"The only price we pay for living in the Big Picture is to hold a bit of doubt and anxiety about the exact how, if, when, where, and who of it all, but never the that." *(p. 111)*

As you reflect on your life, think about whether your religious tradition has or has not helped you to perceive some coherence, purpose, benevolence, and direction in the universe. How has your tradition shaped your view of who God is, what the world is, and where you can expect to find beauty and joy?

_____

_____

_____

_____

_____

_____

"*Either God is for everybody and the divine DNA is somehow in all creatures, or this God is not God by any common definition, or much of a god at all.*"
(*p. 109*)

How do you understand the relationship between those who are in the first half of life and the elders Fr. Richard talks about in this chapter? How would you distinguish someone being an elder socially and an elder spiritually? How have elders in your life assisted you? Are there first-half-of-life people you know for whom you might be an elder? What might you offer to them?

"I now hope and believe
that a kind of second
simplicity is the very goal of
mature adulthood and
mature religion . . . Maybe
that is what several poets
meant when they said 'the
child is father of the man'?"
(p. 108)

What does it mean to you that "simple meaning now suffices"? What is your understanding of the deeper happiness that comes with second-half-of-life wisdom? Have you discovered more significant meaning in your life? What adjectives would you use to describe that meaning? How would you communicate this discovery to someone else, and what would you tell them about the kinds of feelings that it evokes?

"I worry about 'true believers' who cannot carry any doubt or anxiety at all, as Thomas the Apostle and Mother Teresa learned to do . . . To hold the full mystery of life is always to endure its other half, which is the equal mystery of death and doubt."

(pp. 111–112)

Experiential Exercises

• Consider how you are like, rather than unlike, people you tend to oppose. Write a letter to someone whom you would call "other": one who is liberal or one who is conservative, one who believes in the right to abortion or one who believes it is sin, one who is gay or one who condemns homosexuality. Express your insights about how you are just like that person, and try to welcome him or her into your heart. Note your responses to this process. What feelings arose in writing the letter? What biases did it reveal? Were you released from any of them in this process?

• Sit quietly today to contemplate forgiveness. Think back over your life, naming situations in which you wanted forgiveness. Now hold in your awareness those in your life whom you need to forgive. Identify instances when you have passed "sadness, absurdity, judgment, and/or futility" on to others. Hold all of this in your heart, prayerfully inviting

"This new coherence . . . is precisely what gradually characterizes a second-half-of-life person. It feels like a return to simplicity after having learned from all the complexity. Finally, at last, one has lived long enough to see that 'everything belongs,' even the sad absurd and futile parts." (p. 114)

forgiveness and offering it also. Write about how it feels to forgive and to be forgiven. Write also about the circumstances you cannot release in forgiveness, and invite the Holy Spirit to hold those with you.

CHAPTER 10

A Bright Sadness

Our mature years are characterized by a kind of bright sadness and a sober happiness . . . There is still darkness in the second half of life — in fact maybe even more. But there is a changed capacity to hold it creatively and with less anxiety. (p.117)

～ Fr. Richard talks about how in the second half of life, we notice things we share in common with others and don't need to dwell on differences. Have you noticed that too? List the things you have noticed that we all share in common. Are there more or fewer than you expected? How does this focus on things in common help you be more accepting of others' behavior and differences?

_____

_____

_____

_____

_____

_____

_____

_____

_____

_____

_____

_____

"In this second half of life, one has less and less need or interest in eliminating the negative or fearful, making again those old rash judgments, holding on to old hurts or feeling any need to punish other people . . . You fight things only when you are directly called and equipped to do so." (p. 118)

When in your life have you needed to be considered best, superior, the only one God loves, or deserving of superior treatment? Why does such thinking need to be released to move into second half of life thinking?

_____

_____

_____

_____

_____

_____

_____

_____

_____

_____

_____

_____

_____

_____

"*Life is more* participatory *than assertive, and there is no need for strong or further self-definition. God has taken care of all that, much better than we ever expected. The brightness comes from within now, and it is usually more than enough.*" (p. 120)

Generative people believe "their God is no longer small, punitive, or tribal." Erik Erikson defines generative people as those eager and able to generate life from their abundance and for the benefit of following generations. Who do you know who is a generative person? How can you tell? Would you consider yourself to be a generative person? If not, what steps might you take to become more generative?

_____

_____

_____

_____

_____

_____

_____

_____

_____

_____

_____

_____

_____

_____

_____

_____

_____

_____

_____

"*Your concern is not so much* to have what you love *anymore, but to* love what you have—*right now. This is a monumental change . . . , so much so that it is almost the litmus test of whether you are in the second half of life at all.*"
(p. 124)

_____

_____

_____

_____

_____

_____

_____

_____

Fr. Richard says that hoarding, collecting, and impressing others is of less interest to elders. Write about your own desires to hoard, possess, and collect. Do you still feel tempted to try to impress others with your things, your travels, or your life's accomplishments?

_____

_____

_____

_____

_____

_____

_____

_____

_____

_____

_____

_____

_____

"Just watch true elders sitting in any circle of conversation; they are often defining the center, depth, and circumference of the dialogue just by being there. Most participants do not even know it is happening. When elders speak, they need very few words to make their point."

(pp. 119–120)

Experiential Exercises

- Sit for a time and contemplate certainty. Have you noticed that you have fewer moments in your life when you are certain you are right and someone else is wrong? What has replaced your certainty? Write about a situation where you have experienced greater peace by making room for another's view of things rather than a focused attachment to being right. Now write about a situation where you have remained attached to your point of view.

Notice how you feel in your body as you write about the experience of attachment. Notice how you feel in your body as you write about releasing (or being released from) your certainty. Record the sensations of each in your journal.

Invite this awareness to stay with you this week as the next situation arises where your certainty gets in the way of the peace of unknowing. Write about what you experience as you hold this awareness.

"Ironically, we are more than ever before in a position to change people—but we do not need to—and that makes all the difference. We have moved from doing to being to an utterly new kind of doing that flows almost organically, quietly, and by osmosis." (p. 123)

"All of life's problems, dilemmas, and difficulties are now resolved not by negativity, attack, criticism, force, or logical resolution, but always by falling into a larger 'brightness.' This is the falling upward that we have been waiting for! . . . 'The best criticism of the bad is the practice of the better.'" (p. 124)

• Do a solo retreat centered on the Eight Beatitudes. Prepare a space for quiet contemplation. Read the Beatitudes in Matthew 5:3–12 several times, looking for deeper levels of meaning on each reading. How do they apply to your life? Go back to the first one. Perhaps write after each reading, or rewrite the Beatitudes in your own words. Reread what you have written. Move into your week applying the message of the Beatitudes wherever possible. Notice which ones are more difficult for you. Consider why.

CHAPTER 11

The Shadowlands

> Your shadow is what you refuse to see about yourself, and what you do not want others to see... *It is like a double blindness keeping you from seeing—and being—your best and deepest self.* (pp. 127–128)

> *We never get to second half of life without major shadowboxing... It continues until the end of life, the only difference being that you are no longer surprised by your surprises or so totally humiliated by your humiliations!* (p. 131)

⟶ Think about the many roles you play and have played in your life. List the personas you use most often and the rewards you receive from others by projecting them. Are the rewards of living the personas worth the sacrifice of not living as your True Self?

_____

_____

_____

_____

_____

_____

_____

_____

_____

_____

_____

_____

_____

"Holy sadness, once called compunction, is the price your soul pays for opening to the new and the unknown in yourself and in the world. A certain degree of such necessary sadness (another form of necessary suffering!) is important to feel, to accept, and to face."

(p. 135)

Think about how you usually respond to someone who points to your faults or criticizes your actions. Are you able to see the friendship in their challenging message? What might be a helpful phrase to have in your back pocket when you face a challenging message in the future?

Fr. Richard writes, "Spiritual maturity is largely a growth in seeing; and full seeing seems to take most of our lifetime." What do you now see in a different light than you did in the first half of life? What clues do you use to know when you might need to invite a different perspective?

_____

_____

_____

_____

_____

_____

_____

_____

_____

_____

_____

_____

_____

_____

Remembering that your persona is what most people want from you and reward you for, do you notice the difficulties it causes for you and those around you? Identify what you have denied or eliminated to support your persona. Is it comforting to know that your persona or your shadow is not inherently evil? How would you say that your persona allows you to be or do evil and not know it?

_____

_____

_____

_____

_____

_____

_____

_____

_____

_____

_____

_____

_____

_____

_____

_____

"The movement to second-half-of-life wisdom has much to do with necessary shadow work and the emergence of healthy self-critical thinking, which alone allows you to see beyond your own shadow and disguise and to find who you are 'hidden [with Christ] in God,' as Paul puts it (Colossians 3:3)."
(p. 130)

How much shadow boxing have you done as you have grown spiritually? Have you been able to actually see the shadow and its games? Describe something you have identified as a facet of your shadow. Once you named this, what happened to its power over you?

_____

_____

_____

_____

_____

_____

_____

_____

_____

_____

_____

_____

_____

_____

FALLING UPWARD: A COMPANION JOURNAL

Experiential Exercises

• In the week ahead, observe your responses to others. Watch for heightened reactions that may be out of proportion to the moment. As soon as you are able, write a description of the interaction as closely as you remember it. When your reaction has calmed, reread your account of the incident. With compassion, identify the part of your shadow self that was exposed at that point. Reflect on what you have discovered. Invite that piece of your shadow into your heart, and hold it there prayerfully in the coming days.

"Whenever ministers, or any true believers, are too anti anything, you can be pretty sure there is some shadow material lurking somewhere nearby." (p. 128)

• Because the shadow so easily adopts the disguises of righteousness and piety, it can be tricky to spot. In conversations or interactions with your dear ones over the week, listen for fear that might be disguised as prudence or for control disguised as common sense.

"The saint is precisely one who has no 'I' to protect or project . . . Such people do not need to be perfectly right, and they know they cannot be anyway; so they just try to be in right relationship . . . They try above all else to be loving." (p. 132)

Watch for manipulation disguised as justice or for vengeance disguised as "I am doing this for your good." You don't have to try to change anything. Just bring it to your awareness ("There I go again!"), and hold it prayerfully in your heart during your contemplation time this week.

CHAPTER 12

New Problems and New Directions

 The bottom line of the Gospel is that most of us have to hit some kind of bottom before we even start the real spiritual journey. *Up to that point, it is mostly religion. At the bottom, there is little time or interest in being totally practical, efficient, or revenue generating. You just want to breathe fresh air.* (p. 138)

～ Fr. Richard offers this question: "How can I honor the legitimate needs of the first half of life [being practical, efficient, and revenue generating], while creating space, vision, time, and grace for the second?" How would you respond to this question? How will you begin creating the space, vision, time, and grace needed to travel more deeply into the second half of life? Describe how holding the tension between maintaining the container and the contents is the very shape of wisdom.

"In the second half of life, all that you avoided for the sake of a manufactured ego ideal starts coming back as a true friend and teacher. Doers become thinkers, feelers become doers, thinkers become feelers, extroverts become introverts, visionaries become practical, and the practical ones long for vision." *(pp. 148–149)*

As a result of moving toward or into the second half of life, have you felt yourself moving away from groups or friendships? Describe your response to this change. What is your reaction to the concept of being happy alone? How do you respond to the idea that the cure for loneliness is actually solitude?

*"More calm and
contemplative seeing does
not appear suddenly, but
grows almost unconsciously
over many years of conflict,
confusion, healing,
broadening, loving, and
forgiving reality."*

(p. 146)

Write about your understanding of dualistic (either-or) thinking. When has such thinking been useful to you? Describe your understanding of non-dualistic (both-and) thinking. When has this approach been helpful to you? What do you think makes dualistic thinking insufficient for addressing love, suffering, death, God, and infinity?

"*Most people do not see things as they* are, *rather they see things as* they *are. In my experience, this is most of the world, unless people have done their inner work, at least some shadow work, and thereby entered into wisdom, or nondualistic thinking.*"
(p. 148)

As you go through your day, try to observe examples of both dualistic and nondualistic thinking in your thought. Do you notice that both-and thinking relieves you of the need to divide or judge? Think about how both-and thinking can help you to deal with family and friends, issues at work, or political debates. How can such thinking help you to move freely from contemplation to skillful action?

What does it mean to see "in wholes" and no longer "in parts"? What "messy parts" have you had to delve into to reach for wholeness? Has falling back into those parts brought you home to yourself more fully?

Experiential Exercises

• Fr. Richard writes, "The human art form is in uniting fruitful activity with a contemplative stance — not one or the other, but always both at the same time." Write about what you understand this to mean. Identify and list the fruitful activities in your life. What clues do you have to point to whether they are or are not rooted in contemplation? Can you tell by the stance underlying them? How you feel when you are participating in them?

• At the end of your contemplative times this week, sit with your journal and note any urgings of your spirit. Is the silence calling you to something?

• Identify someone in your life whom you would call soulful, that is, someone who reflects a sense of abundance, grace, and freedom. Notice how their calm and their peace affect those around them. Talk to this person about how he or she views conflict and what he or she does to bring calm and peace to these kinds of situations. Ask how he or she opens up options and alternatives. Can you identify any of these qualities in yourself? Have you become aware

of some qualities you would like to try on? How might you live into some of these behaviors and attitudes more fully? Practice some of these in your daily life this week, and write about what happens.

CHAPTER 13

Falling Upward

What looks like falling can largely be experienced as falling upward and onward, into a broader and deeper world, where the soul has found its fullness, is finally connected to the whole, and lives inside the Big Picture. (p. 153)

Fr. Richard says that great people come to serve, not to be served. How have you come to serve? Does the list of those you serve include people other than your family and friends? How can you "give your life away"?

_____

_____

_____

_____

_____

_____

_____

_____

_____

_____

_____

_____

_____

_____

_____

Are you able to name one or two friends who have been a true mirror for you? If so, write a note to the friend expressing your thanks and explaining why you are so grateful. If your one true mirror has been the accepting gaze of God, write a prayer of thanksgiving for that gift.

"*It is only those who respond to the real you,* good or bad, *that help you in the long run. Much of the work of midlife is learning to tell the difference between people who are still dealing with their issues through you and those who are really dealing with you as you really are.*" *(p. 155)*

How does mirroring work? How were you mirrored as a child? How are you being mirrored in adulthood? List the many relational, professional, emotional, and physical falls. Next to each entry write what happened following that fall. In retrospect, do you see a bouncing upward after those falls? If so, describe what that was like and how you changed.

↝ Notice the times in the fallings you listed in the previous reflection where the problem was within the solution. If you place yourself inside some of Jesus' parables, do you see your life experiences in a different light? As you reflect on your life, think about which of your major problems blossomed and became your solutions.

"Like good spiritual directors do, God must say after each failure of ours, 'Oh, here is a great opportunity! Let's see how we can work with this!' After our ego-inflating successes, God surely says, 'Well, nothing new or good is going to happen here.'"
(p. 158)

~ Fr. Richard writes, "Like any true mirror, the gaze of God receives us exactly as we are, without judgment or distortion, subtraction or addition. Such *perfect receiving* is what transforms us." What feelings does this statement evoke? Have there been times when you've felt this perfect receiving from God? If so, have you seen its power to transform you? If not, try to identify what is blocking you from opening this gift from God.

"Good people will mirror goodness in us, which is why we love them so much. Not-so-mature people will mirror their own unlived and confused life onto us, which is why they confuse and confound us so much, and why they are so hard to love." *(p. 155)*

FALLING UPWARD: A COMPANION JOURNAL

Experiential Exercises

Read about or watch a movie on the life of Helen Keller. Observe how and when she moves from first to second half of life. Reflect on why and how she may have found life's joy and how she developed the generativity for others for which she is famous. How does Helen Keller's example inspire you to find new ways to serve others?

"In the second half of life, people have less power to infatuate you, but they also have much less power to control you or hurt you. It is the freedom of the second half not to need."
(pp. 157–158)

Write a letter to yourself as the person who has come through your falling-apart life experiences. Even if you are in the midst of them now, embrace the viewpoint of the one who has fallen upward. In the process, finally let go of whatever difficulties you have been lamenting. Be both compassionate and completely honest. Spell out what you need to let go of and write about how that letting go will affect you

"God will always give you exactly what you truly want and desire. So make sure you desire, desire deeply, desire yourself, desire God, desire everything good, true, and beautiful." (p. 160)

and others. Write about the fact that "pain in life is part of the deal." Offer the letter to God as your prayer for healing.

Fr. Richard Rohr is a globally recognized ecumenical teacher bearing witness to the universal awakening within mystical and transformational traditions. A Franciscan priest of the New Mexico Province and founder of the Center for Action and Contemplation (CAC) in Albuquerque, New Mexico, his teaching is grounded in practices of contemplation and lived *kenosis* (self-emptying), expressing itself in radical compassion, particularly for the socially marginalized.

Fr. Richard is the author of numerous books, including *The Naked Now*, *Everything Belongs*, *Adam's Return*, *Breathing Under Water*, and *Falling Upward*.

CAC is home to the Rohr Institute and its Living School for Action and Contemplation. Fr. Richard is available to speak to groups convening in the New Mexico area. To learn more about the school, visit www.cac.org.

Falling Upward

A Spirituality for the Two Halves of Life

"Understanding the spiritual aspects of
aging is as important as appreciating the
systems and biological processes that age us.
Richard Rohr has given us a perfect guide
to what he calls the 'further journey,'
a voyage into the mystery and beauty of
healthy spiritual maturity."
—Mehmet Oz, M.D., host of the
"Dr. Oz Show"

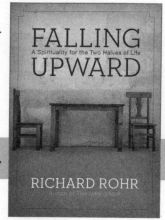

**Hardcover | 240 p
$19.95 | 978-0-470-90775-7**

In *Falling Upward*, Father Richard Rohr—the founder of
the Center for Action and Contemplation—offers a new
paradigm for understanding one of the most profound of
life's mysteries: how our failings can be the foundation for
our ongoing spiritual growth. Drawing on the wisdom
from time-honored myths, heroic poems, great thinkers,
and sacred religious texts, the author explores the two
halves of life to show that those who have fallen, failed, or
"gone down" are the only ones who understand "up." We
grow spiritually more by doing it wrong than by doing it
right.

Immortal Diamond

The Search for Our True Self

January 2013 | Hardcover
$19.95 | 9781118303597

If there's a False Self, is there also a True Self?

What is it? How is it found? Why does it matter?

And what does it have to do with the spiritual journey?

In *Immortal Diamond*, Rohr likens True Self to a diamond, buried deep within us, formed under the intense pressure of our lives, that must be searched for, uncovered, separated from all the debris of ego that surrounds it. In a sense True Self must, like Jesus, be resurrected, and that process is not resuscitation but transformation.

Immortal Diamond (whose title is taken from a line in a poem by Gerard Manley Hopkins) explores the deepest questions of identity, spirituality, and meaning in Richard Rohr's inimitable style.

Center for Action and Contemplation

Home of THE ROHR INSTITUTE

The Center for Action and Contemplation was founded by Fr. Richard Rohr, O.F.M in 1987. Located in its original South Valley neighborhood in Albuquerque, New Mexico, it exemplifies the Franciscans' 800-year tradition of remaining visible and interactive in a highly populated and secular community.

The Center is home to the Rohr Institute, which draws upon the Franciscan alternative orthodoxy, emphasizing practice over dogma. Its programs, including the Living School, bear witness to an ecumenical and inclusive Christianity grounded within its mystical traditions. The Center's education mission is to produce compassionate and powerfully learned individuals who will work for positive change in the world based on compassion for the suffering and an awareness of our common union with Divine Reality and all beings.

Are you ready to conspire for change?

LĪVING SCHOOL *for*
Action *and* Contemplation

Grounded in the Christian mystical tradition

Empowering individuals for compassionate action

Acknowledging our differences

Valuing our one-ness

That all may be one. – John 17:21

Learn more about the two-year program
and on-line courses at

www.cac.org